# Winter Wedding Guest Book

 # In Celebration of

_____

Date                                    Location
_____

# Our Wedding Party

## Best Man

_____

## Groomsmen

_____

_____

_____

_____

# Our Wedding Party

## Maid of Honor

_____

## Bridesmaids

_____
_____
_____
_____
_____

Flower Girl

Ring Bearer

Ushers

# Guest Name & Address

# Thoughts & Best Wishes

# Guest Name & Address

# Thoughts & Best Wishes

# Guest Name & Address

# Thoughts & Best Wishes

# Guest Name & Address

# Thoughts & Best Wishes

## Guest Name & Address

# Thoughts & Best Wishes

# Guest Name & Address

# Thoughts & Best Wishes

# Guest Name & Address

# Thoughts & Best Wishes

# Guest Name & Address

# Thoughts & Best Wishes

# Guest Name & Address

# Thoughts & Best Wishes

# Guest Name & Address

# Thoughts & Best Wishes

# Guest Name & Address

# Thoughts & Best Wishes

# Guest Name & Address

# Thoughts & Best Wishes

## Guest Name & Address

# Thoughts & Best Wishes

# Guest Name & Address

# Thoughts & Best Wishes

# Guest Name & Address

# Thoughts & Best Wishes

# Guest Name & Address

# Thoughts & Best Wishes

# Guest Name & Address

# Thoughts & Best Wishes

# Guest Name & Address

# Thoughts & Best Wishes

# Guest Name & Address

# Thoughts & Best Wishes

## Guest Name & Address

# Thoughts & Best Wishes

# Guest Name & Address

# Thoughts & Best Wishes

# Guest Name & Address

# Thoughts & Best Wishes

# Guest Name & Address

# Thoughts & Best Wishes

# Guest Name & Address

# Thoughts & Best Wishes

# Guest Name & Address

# Thoughts & Best Wishes

# Guest Name & Address

# Thoughts & Best Wishes

# Guest Name & Address

# Thoughts & Best Wishes

# Guest Name & Address

# Thoughts & Best Wishes

# Guest Name & Address

# Thoughts & Best Wishes

# Guest Name & Address

# Thoughts & Best Wishes

# Guest Name & Address

# Thoughts & Best Wishes

# Guest Name & Address

# Thoughts & Best Wishes

# Guest Name & Address

# Thoughts & Best Wishes

# Guest Name & Address

# Thoughts & Best Wishes

# Guest Name & Address

# Thoughts & Best Wishes

# Guest Name & Address

# Thoughts & Best Wishes

# Guest Name & Address

# Thoughts & Best Wishes

# Guest Name & Address

# Thoughts & Best Wishes

# Guest Name & Address

# Thoughts & Best Wishes

# Guest Name & Address

# Thoughts & Best Wishes

# Guest Name & Address

# Thoughts & Best Wishes

# Guest Name & Address

# Thoughts & Best Wishes

# Guest Name & Address

# Thoughts & Best Wishes

# Guest Name & Address

# Thoughts & Best Wishes

# Guest Name & Address

# Thoughts & Best Wishes

# Guest Name & Address

# Thoughts & Best Wishes

# Guest Name & Address

# Thoughts & Best Wishes

## Guest Name & Address

# Thoughts & Best Wishes

# Guest Name & Address

# Thoughts & Best Wishes

# Guest Name & Address

# Thoughts & Best Wishes

# Guest Name & Address

# Thoughts & Best Wishes

# Guest Name & Address

# Thoughts & Best Wishes

# Guest Name & Address

# Thoughts & Best Wishes

# Guest Name & Address

# Thoughts & Best Wishes

# Guest Name & Address

# Thoughts & Best Wishes

# Guest Name & Address

# Thoughts & Best Wishes

# Guest Name & Address

# Thoughts & Best Wishes

# Guest Name & Address

www.ingramcontent.com/pod-product-compliance
Lightning Source LLC
LaVergne TN
LVHW060334080526
838202LV00053B/4472